FARM ANIMALS

Pigs

Jared Siemens

LET'S READ
AV²
BY WEIGL™
ADDED VALUE • AUDIO VISUAL

Go to **www.av2books.com**, and enter this book's unique code.

BOOK CODE

AVJ88963

AV² by Weigl brings you media enhanced books that support active learning.

AV² provides enriched content that supplements and complements this book. Weigl's AV² books strive to create inspired learning and engage young minds in a total learning experience.

Your AV² Media Enhanced books come alive with...

Audio
Listen to sections of the book read aloud.

Video
Watch informative video clips.

Embedded Weblinks
Gain additional information for research.

Try This!
Complete activities and hands-on experiments.

Key Words
Study vocabulary, and complete a matching word activity.

Quizzes
Test your knowledge.

Slide Show
View images and captions, and prepare a presentation.

... and much, much more!

Published by AV² by Weigl
350 5th Avenue, 59th Floor New York, NY 10118
Website: www.av2books.com

Library of Congress Cataloging-in-Publication Data

Names: Siemens, Jared, author.
Title: Pigs / Jared Siemens.
Description: New York, NY : Published by AV² by Weigl, 2018. | Series: Farm animals | Includes index.
Identifiers: LCCN 2018050064 (print) | LCCN 2018051560 (ebook) | ISBN 9781489695383 (Multi User Ebook) | ISBN 9781489695390 (Single User Ebook) | ISBN 9781489695369 (hardcover : alk. paper) | ISBN 9781489695376 (softcover : alk. paper)
Subjects: LCSH: Swine--Juvenile literature.
Classification: LCC SF395.5 (ebook) | LCC SF395.5 .S54 2018 (print) | DDC 636.4--dc23
LC record available at https://lccn.loc.gov/2018050064

Printed in Guangzhou, China
1 2 3 4 5 6 7 8 9 0 22 21 20 19 18

122018
102918

Art Director: Terry Paulhus   Project Coordinator: Jared Siemens

Weigl acknowledges Getty Images, iStock, Shutterstock, and Alamy as the primary image suppliers for this title.

Pigs

In this book you will learn

how they look

what they do

what they eat

why we keep them

and much more!

Pigs

A pig is a large farm animal.

Farmers keep pigs for food.

Iowa has more pigs than any other state.

A baby pig
is called
a piglet.

Piglets weigh about 3 pounds when they are born.

A fully grown pig can weigh up to **700 pounds.**

Pigs have four short legs and a curled tail.

Their bodies are covered with short hair.

Pigs have large
noses called snouts.

They have a great
sense of smell.

Pigs use
their snouts
to dig and
look for food.

Pigs know each other by smell.

They can form friendships like people do.

Pigs talk to each other mostly with squeals and grunts.

A pig can make up to 20 different sounds.

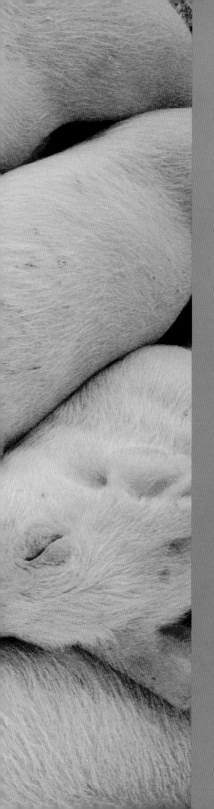

Pigs are very
clean animals.

A pig will not make
a mess where it eats
or sleeps.

Pigs are one of the smartest animals on Earth.

They learn fast and can remember things.

Farmers keep pigs in large and muddy spaces.

Rolling in the mud helps pigs stay cool.

PIG FACTS

These pages provide detailed information that expands on the interesting facts found in the book. They are intended to be used by adults as a learning support to help young readers round out their knowledge of each unique animal featured in the *Farm Animals* series and why it is kept and raised on farms.

Pages 4–5

A pig is a large farm animal. Pigs can be brown, black, white, or pink. Farmers feed pigs a diet of corn and barley to help them grow. United States farmers raise more than 115 million pigs each year for meat. On average, there are about 20 million pigs being raised by farmers in Iowa at any given time.

Pages 6–7

A baby pig is called a piglet. Piglets weigh about 2 to 4 pounds (1 to 2 kilograms) at birth. They grow very quickly, doubling their birth weight in just one week. Piglets drink their mother's milk for their first three weeks of life and are weaned around 1 month of age. Adult pigs can weigh between 300 and 700 pounds (136 and 317.5 kg).

Pages 8–9

Pigs have four short legs and a curled tail. A pig's hair is thick and bristly, similar to a hairbrush. This thick hair helps keep pigs warm during winter. A pig has four short legs with very hard hooves on each foot. Curled tails are more pronounced in domesticated pigs than in pigs found in nature.

Pages 10–11

Pigs have large noses called snouts. The snout is the most sensitive part of a pig's body. Pigs have an excellent sense of smell thanks to their large, leathery noses. A pig will use its snout to help it find both food and other pigs. In France, pigs are trained to find and dig up expensive, edible fungi called truffles.

Pigs know each other by smell. Every pig develops its own unique smell due to environmental factors, such as where it sleeps and what it eats. Pigs can tell each other apart by this unique smell. Pigs develop strong friendships, and will spend most of their time with just a few other pigs.

Pigs love to talk to one another. Pigs may talk to one another by grunting, barking, squealing, or snorting. A pig will bark to warn another pig of danger. Pigs usually squeal when they are hungry or upset. Pig squeals can be louder than a jet engine at takeoff.

Pigs are very clean animals. Pigs have earned a reputation for being messy, mostly because of their love of mud. However, pigs are very clean animals, and prefer water to mud for cooling themselves down. One pig owner created a special shower for her pigs to use, and they learned how to turn it on and off on their own.

Pigs are one of the smartest animals on Earth. Scientists assert that a pig is likely smarter than the average 3-year-old human. Some pigs have even learned to play video games. Pigs have also been observed tricking each another in an effort to get more food.

Farmers keep pigs in large and muddy spaces. Pigs cannot sweat, which means they have to use their environment to help stay cool. Farmers keep pigs in shaded areas or in places where the pigs can access water or mud to bathe in. When you see a pig rolling the mud, it is cooling itself off.

KEY WORDS

Research has shown that as much as 65 percent of all written material published in English is made up of 300 words. These 300 words cannot be taught using pictures or learned by sounding them out. They must be recognized by sight. This book contains 55 common sight words to help young readers improve their reading fluency and comprehension. This book also teaches young readers several important content words, such as proper nouns. These words are paired with pictures to aid in learning and improve understanding.

Page	Sight Words First Appearance
4	a, animal, farm, food, for, is, keep, large
5	any, has, more, other, state, than
7	about, are, can, they, to, up, when
8	and, four, have, their, with
10	great, look, of, use
12	by, each, know
13	do, like, people
14	different, make, sounds, talk
17	eats, it, not, or, very, where, will
18	Earth, learn, on, one, the, things
21	helps, in

Page	Content Words First Appearance
4	farmers, pig
5	Iowa
6	piglet
7	pounds
8	bodies, hair, legs, tail
10	noses, sense, snouts
13	friendships
14	grunts, squeals
21	mud, spaces

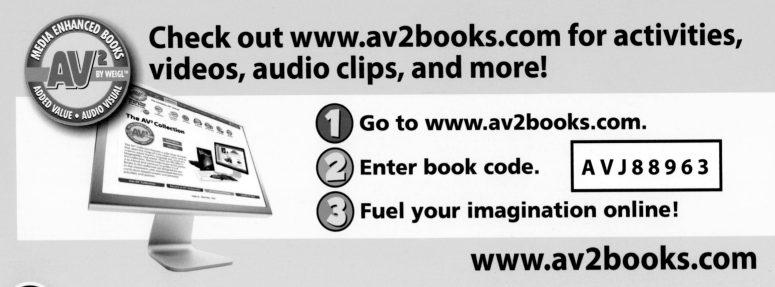